THE COLORS OF HAIRS

by R Marion Rock
Illustrated by Nancy Cox

Sarah,
Wishing you all
the best on your
21st birthday!
Love, Aunt Claire

The Colors of Haiku
© Copyright 2004 R Marion Rock and Nancy Cox

Haiku

Haiku, a Japanese verse form, notable for its compression and suggestiveness, consists of three unrhymed lines of five, seven and five syllables.

Ideally, a haiku presents a pair of contrasting images, one suggestive of time and place, the other a vivid but fleeting observation. Working together, they evoke mood and emotion. The poet does not comment on the connection but leaves the synthesis of the two images for the reader to perceive.

The haiku evolved from the earlier link-versed form known as the renga and was used extensively by Zen Buddhist monks in the 15th and 16th centuries. In the next 200 years, the verse form achieved its greatest popularity and success.

The concise nature of the haiku influenced the early 20th-century Anglo-American poetic movement known as Imagism. The writing of haiku is still practiced by thousands who annually publish outstanding examples in the many magazines devoted to the art.

This book combines Rock's haiku with the imagery of Nancy Cox, taking both expressions to a heightened level of synergy and beauty.

My chosen profession contains many positive aspects, not the least being the many wonderful people with whom I've been privileged to meet and work. In thinking about the way that Bob Rock and I have come to be working partners, I do realize that it has been nothing short of amazing.

Friends of mine had commissioned me to do a painting of their house. Bob was at their place, inquiring about a possible rental. He talked about his writing and that he was interested in finding an artist to do illustrative work. My friend showed Bob the painting I had done. Shortly after that I was with the same friend in front of a local bookstore. We were quickly introduced and I just happened to have an invitation to the exhibit where my work was hanging at that time. Bob kindly took the card from me and proceeded to go see the work. After viewing the paintings he began to think that his writing coupled with my artistic vision might just be a match.

I am so inspired by Bob's sensitive, and at times, witty writing. The images I need come easily to mind. It is my desire that our team effort brings you delight.

Nancy Cox

Dedication

My words are dedicated to my children, whom I admire, who have been my teachers, whom I love for many reasons, (one of which is for allowing me to be weird), whose laughter remains the greatest joy in my life…and whom I like as much as I love.

R Marion Rock

FLORA'S WHISPER

PRISM SOUL WITHIN

SPEAKS OF LIFETIMES MOMENTS OLD

NOT ITS DESTINE FEARS

BUTTERFLY

HEAVEN'S SILKEN KITE

WINGS DIRECT A SILENT SONG

FLOATS ABOUT AWAY

ODE TO THE SUMAC

NOR FLOWER NOR BOUGH

SUMMER'S WANE FIRST AUTUMN'S KISS

PLUMED DELIGHT FOREBODES

ME AND MY BEST PLANT

GIVE THE PLANT A DRINK
I THINK I HAVE HAD ENOUGH
WE SHALL BOTH SOON WILT

EASY FRIENDS

HOME MOST ANYWHERE

FURRY BOY AND BOY-LIKE DOG

GRANDPA'S YESTERYEAR

ROAD TO TOMORROW

TRAIL INTO AUTUMN
NO JUDGEMENT ON SEASONS PAST
LIGHT WILL SHOW THE WAY

PILLOWING

MORNING DEW GLISTENS

WHISPERS SOFTLY OF THE NIGHT

HEART PRINTS FOR THE DAY

YOUTH

FLEETING MOMENTS GONE

QUILT OF DREAMS TO KEEP ONE SAFE

WASTED ON THE YOUNG

THE MOUNTAIN

OUTSPREAD SHOULDERED REEF

SUMMIT TOUCHING HEAVEN'S STAIR

BEAUTY NONPAREILS

MS. SPIDER

ACROBATIC QUEEN

WEAVING ONE OF NATURE'S QUILTS

DINNER SOON IS SERVED

FOG

YOU SHROUD YOU BLANKET

DARKNESS CANNOT HIDE YOUR SOUL

WITH SUN NOW BEGONE

THE SEA

ANCIENT MOTHER'S WOMB

EON'S ERE NOW MAN'S FIRST SEED

RESTLESS CLAMORS CALM

TIME

SNOWFLAKE IN OUR HAND

QUESTIONING A THOUGHT A DEED

MELTING UNFULFILLED

THE RABBIT

POWDER PUFF AT REAR
A LITTLE BUNNY FOO FOO
SHOULD HAVE BEAT THE SHELL

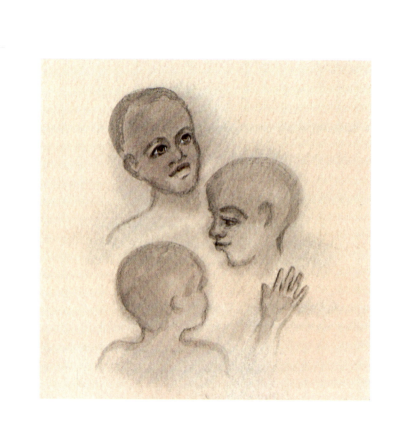

GIFT OF INNOCENTS

CHILDREN OF THE DIRT

KINDRED SPIRITS REACHING OUT

NOT TO REAP BUT SOW

CORAL MOON

NIGHT TO DAY SO FULL

SEDUCE ONCE MORE CORAL SQUIRE

ROUND WAFT CIRCLE ROUND

BE STILL

BARREN MOTHER SLEEPS

PROMISES ARE DREAMED THEN KEPT

QUIET NOW BE STILL

THE OAK

TWELVE THOUSAND MOONS PAST

PROVIDE YOUR SHADOW SPLENDOR

LIFETIMES JUST BEGUN

INFANT SPIRIT

A STAR IS BORN FREE

GOING WHERE IT WILL CARRY

BRIGHT AS IT MAY SHINE

RIVER BEING

MIGHTY RAINDROP FALLS

CLEANSING ONLY THIS TIME 'ROUND

SEARCHING FOR THE SEA

THE CANDLE

BRAVE LONE DANCING FIRE

EACH FLICKER FROM YEARS GONE PAST

BIRTH A MOMENT'S PEACE

NO SERENDIPITY

WASN'T MEANT TO BE

THE FATES CHOSE TO LOOK AWAY

BACK TO YESTERDAY

SWING

MY NO GRAVITY

OH MY THERE IT IS AGAIN

GRAVITY ABOUNDS

THE KISS

KISS SWEETLY PRECIOUS
SCENT OF LINGERING BLOSSOMS
SINGS NIGHTINGALE'S SONG

THUNDER

HEAVEN'S CHORUS SINGS

RUMBLING TRAIN ACROSS THE GRAY

STIRRING MOTHER'S NESTS

IN LOVE

ONE TOUCH ANOTHER

THE FIRST TIME EVERY TIME

LOVE LOVING LIKING

MIGHTY ACACIA

HORIZON'S SHADOW
MAN'S WHISPER MARA'S THUNDER
STALWART STAFF PRESIDES

FIREFLY

FLYING TINY STAR

DANCING PINBALL IN THE DARK

TWINKLE AND YOU'RE GONE

SUNRISE

ETERNAL CANDLE

PRISM PATH ACROSS THE SEA

NOBLE PILOT ORB

BALLOON

BUBBLE ON A STRING

A DELIGHTFUL RAINBOW MOON

CHILDREN'S FACES GLOW

MAPLE'S GLOW

GOLDEN PLUMAGE SIGHS
SUNSET BOSSES PETALS FALL
SETTING NOW AWAITS

LAST LEAF OF AUTUMN

LEAVES OF AUTUMN DOWN

UNTO MOTHER'S WOMB RETURN

ONCE MORE COMPASS CROWNED

BON VOYAGE

NINETY THINGS TO SAY
NOT YET SPOKEN LEFT UNSAID
JUST BYEKU BYEKU

ABOUT THE WRITER

Writer, poet, songwriter, R Marion Rock is also the author of *Children's Stories Mermaid's Tears*, *The First Firefly - A Christmas Story* and *An Ornament for Renee*. Other of Rock's writings have contributed to the successful publication of *Voices from Vietnam*. Other poetry has been published in *Spirits in Motion*. Rock, a member of the Wisconsin Fellowship of Poets, has 3 children and 4 grandchildren and resides in Madison, Wisconsin. He can be contacted by e-mail through www.colorsofverse.com.

ABOUT THE ARTIST

Nancy Cox works in watercolor, painting on location in and around her rural Black Earth, Wisconsin studio. Illustrating a book has been a life-long dream. This is her first book. She would like to dedicate it to her beautiful family— her artist husband Gary, son Matthew and daughter Emily.